Fireflies

Bisera Dalcheska Taleska

Presentation by *BookLeaf Publishing*

Web: www.bookleafpub.com

E-mail: info@bookleafpub.com

ISBN: 9789358313246

First edition 2023

Dedicated to my beloved daughter, Mila.

May you always walk with unwavering strength through life, knowing that you'll always have a home in me.

Fireflies

Late-night thoughts of fireflies
Take me back to a village
Where I ran, barefoot, on dew-kissed grass.

Born in the aftermath of Yugoslavia's
dissolution,
I grew up amidst stories of Tito,
"Nobody can compare to Tito."

Pictures of him hanging in every home,
As if he were part of each family,
My young self yearned to hear more.

Ethnic tensions, war conflicts followed,
"Macedonia for Macedonians," echoed,
As I took the first steps towards the municipal
school.

Fists clashed in the schoolyard,
Division, tension,
"I am not afraid, I am not afraid," we, neighbors.

Neighbors divided in the schoolyards,
Thoughts of winning,
But winning what?

Our town, our playground,
Our school, our cobbled streets,
Marred with anger and rage.

A Gypsy

"You'll never be any better than this gypsy girl
here,"
My Macedonian language and literature teacher
spat.
Heat rushed to my cheeks, fiery red,
Eyes fell to the cracked classroom floor,
Fingers clenched, I became deaf to the rest.

"You'll never be any better than this gypsy girl
here,"
What would my mother say? My father?
No more than a gypsy girl? Me?
My first year of middle school,
I am no more than... wait.

I glanced at her smirking smile,
And dug my nails into the tender skin beneath
my left thumb.
Gripped by my mother's expectations,
I went completely silent.

More than a decade went by,
Walking in the park with my baby girl in her
stroller.
There she stood, the Gypsy girl.

Twin girls in dresses walking by her side.
Our eyes met, shared a greeting, smiles, and
laughter.
A joke about time's swift flight
And we, both now mothers.
Mothers.

We exchanged glances for our daughters,
Eyes filled with love and warmth.

"You'll never be any..."
Never let me be.

Mulberry Tree

For my Grandfather

A 'Wine and Design' night out,
An artist's brush, a blank canvas, and a lousy
attempt
To paint the white mulberry tree
That stands right at the entrance of the yard.

Every stroke, a feeling evoked.
Crimson hues for the fence,
Serene blue for the spring under the tree,
A patch of green for the grass.
Brown for the wooden swing,
That, once, used to sway.
White dots for the mulberries on the tree,
Yellow, in the upper right corner,
For all the hellebores we would seek.

All the laughter, I cannot paint,
Nor the joy of when the accordion was played,
I can paint a willow tree
To show how much your absence means to me.

America's Cry

In classrooms, teachers are pleading,
For more than just cash,
Recognition, real parenting, backing.
Yet, more students, more demands, more papers
to fill,
When's enough gonna be enough?

Line workers, weary, sore feet and hands,
Seek acknowledgment each day,
Better pay, some rest.
A slice of pizza is what they get.
When's enough gonna be enough?

Nurses, stressed and burnt out,
Caring souls,
Endless hours, piles of papers, they shout.
In this lack of support, stress piles high,
When's enough gonna be enough?

On the lonely roads, truck drivers roll,
Missing birthdays, holidays, movie nights at
home.
They dream of life beyond this
Endless grind,
When's enough gonna be enough?

In the bustling kitchens, restaurant workers
hustle,
Low pay, chaotic schedules,
Late nights, weekends,
Another job piled on the heap,
When's enough gonna be enough?

Pregnant women, carrying life's precious load,
Drowning in medical bills,
Heading back to work so soon after birth,
Juggling diapers, bottles, pumps, and sleepless
nights.
When's enough gonna be enough?

Sick folks, in this unending wait,
Hospitals loom large, their stories hard to tell.
No insurance, no money,
Backs against the wall,
When's enough gonna be enough?

They ask, and the tears fall.

Tempest

Grabbing a cup of coffee together was the intent,
Coffee turned into beer, and you knocked me off
my feet.
Elizabeth and Darcy's love was nowhere in my
scene,
So, the passion we shared was enough for me.

The summer slipped away in seconds,
The nights stretched longer, the air got crispier,
You shook my world to pieces,
As the nights trembled with desire.

In the whirlwind of laughter and tears,
I closed my eyes countless times.
While I wished for a tender dance,
Caught in a tempest, I was swept away.

Like a new dawn rising after a moonless night,
New hope was born in the two faint lines -
Another heart pounding in my chest.

In a world that should cradle, I stood exposed
and frail.
And he, once a protector, became a hollow hill.
Words, like shards of glass, pierced through,

When I longed for warmth and shelter.

Within the darkness,
I found my strength,
Resilience born from solitude.

I now hold my own light.

Wheelbarrow Queen

In the cornfield, I'd lose myself for days,
Playing pretend, lost in a childhood maze.
Running through tall stalks,
Imagining a savior, dreaming of adventures.
My arms would get drizzled by the leaves,
Then, I'd pick a few,
Make a doll or just break them along the veins.
Near Grandpa's cornfield, a house nearby,
I'd wander over to drink from the stream.
In it, a watermelon cools,
In rural Balkan corners, this was the way.
Drinking from the spring, I'd peek inside the
house beside the corn.
My heart, curious and wide,
Eager to explore the world inside.
An old lady would come to me,
Offer bread with margarine on top.
On the way home my grandpa would put me in
the wheelbarrow
On top of hay or corn,
And I'd become the wheelbarrow queen.

Thirties

Looking at my to-do lists, and my far-fetched plans,
My repetitive schedule, and my everyday routine,
I think about all the times I did something for the final time.
I think about the last morning I woke up in my childhood bed,
Then, the last time my mother's breakfast was awaiting me,
And the last time all the 90s kids ventured out to play.
When I gaze into my daughter's eyes,
I can't help but think about the last time she fell asleep on my chest,
And the time when, in my arms, she drifted off to dream.
All these fractions of time, not realizing that a moment might be a last.

In my thirtieth year of life on Earth, I feel like a river,
Slowly flowing, devoid of expectations, be it good or bad,
A few rocks in my way, then a smooth ride,
Until I evolve into a waterfall, and I let it be.

Breathlessness

Being trapped in an anxious body is,
An urgent summon to sweep the floors,
And a new microfiber cloth to wipe the dust.
Restless nights until exhaustion cradles you,
Only to be startled by your pounding heart.
In the middle of a meeting, you grapple with
shallow breaths.
Entering places, clutching a pen, a bag,
Or the hemline of your sweater,
As if you're going to get squished by others,
Yet you wear a painted smile, small talk, and
nod politely.
On certain days, it's as if an elephant's sitting on
your chest,
Counting blessings fails to mend it.
A smokey room, and you wave your hand before
you,
Attempting to disperse the fog. And, some days,
you succeed.
Thoughts race like shoes in a drying cycle,
Tumbling and bouncing around, hitting the
sides,
Until, at last, a deep breath is drawn.
Breathing anxiously, or anxiously breathing.

Baby Girl

In the heart of the Balkan, my ob-gyn
I'd see,
A seasoned lady,
She'd share a joke, then delve into my life,
Marriage, duties, financial chat.
Then, with a smile, she'd end each
visit.
Until one day, she made it clear,
"Rest assured, young one, you'll have another
one to
   bear."
In Balkan society, it seemed, the highest
   delight,
Was to bear a son, their measure of might.

My daughter's presence,
   A blessing,
My heart singing, ecstatic to welcome
A girl into my life.

Diner Love

We sit in the diner right across,
I see the napkins and I imagine
J.K. Rowling grabbing a few,
Writing her thoughts down,
And there it is – boom.
Then, I see you there, tense,
And vividly stressed,
Talking of America's hypocrisy
When fueling wars.

As we wait for dinner in the diner right across,
I think of all the times we've sat like this;
Your eyes undressing me,
My fingers tracing a path from your shoulder
down.
My head rests against your cheek,
I lean on you,
You lean on me.
I see the vulnerable child behind your bars,
You see the dreamer in my stoic stance.

I wish for a cottage in the woods,
Away from this all. I blink –
I see you starting a fire,
A fire, then a fire of love,

Smells like you and tobacco,
Burnt wood, and –
Smothered chicken and mashed potatoes,
Southern dinner in the diner right across.
Still, I love you.

In Secret

After my grandpa died,
My grandma got herself a nice suit,
Washed it, ironed it,
Meticulously hung it in the wooden wardrobe.
I'd go up the stairs to her room,
In secret,
Look, for a while, at the suit,
And wonder how one prepares for
Death.
Eventually, opening its door
Would fill the air with a strong mothball smell.
In a drawer right under the TV,
Grandpa's Old Spice stayed long after his death.
In secret,
I'd take it out and smell it.

My mom and dad told me he had gone to
Heaven.
I often thought about death afterward;
First, it was Heaven or Hell,
Then, it became Nonsense,
Worms eating away your flesh,
Until it became an absolute calmness,
Stillness, and quietness, all around.
The first night must be the hardest.

Macedonia Unbound

Borders shifted, changed name, identity
shattered,
The Union, and its peers, a complex work of art,
Keep on making decisions from afar.
The people's voice unheard
For the land where Aleksandar's legacy stood.

With the Agreements' ink, Macedonia's fate,
Sealed, scarred, and torn apart.
Heavier than the Ottoman rule,
Divisions and wars fueled by foreign forces,
Igniting a fire between its people.

Hopelessness, poverty, despair, and corruption,
Rule in the cradle of Slavic literacy.
Attempting to extinguish the flame,
The right to be is denied,
With your sly deals, disguised as hope.

Like a tormented prisoner for centuries,
Suffering the blows of oppressive policies,
Enduring abuse, it still stands.
Longing for a dawn of liberation, when each link
bursts open -
Macedonia released from the shackles of
oppression.

Ashes

Is it too late to reinvent myself?
To become all,
And none.
Become a cat lady,
And a nightguard.
Start rolling tobacco,
And drink sugarless Turkish coffee.
Grab a newspaper
And skim it on my Ikea chair
On a balcony in Avignon.
Dye my hair inky black
And become a pub singer in Dingle;
"Mush-a ring dumb-a do dumb-a da
Whack fall the daddy-o, whack fall the
daddy-o."
Buy a boat in Gloucester,
And live off fishing;
"Fair winds and following seas."
Become a librarian in the Real Gabinete
Portugues de Leitura,
And artfully weave knowledge and exhibits.
Is it too late to reinvent myself?
Start breathing, fully, deeply,
Fear not that whatever I touch may turn into
Ashes.

Comeback

Anger and heartache explode in the
     pit of my stomach,
Expectations drive me to the
     edge of a cliff.

A raging storm outside,
I hear the rain thumping on my
     window pane,
It used to ease me down -
My arms are numb, my face is still.

I come back to a simple moment -
A not-so-fresh cup of coffee,
Atwood's novel on the side table,
Dust on the TV stand,
Carrots ready to be cut.

     Smile, for Christ's sake.
Bitten cuticles, spotless home,
Watery eyes, neatly packed closet.

     Panic attacks.

My geraniums crave water.
     So do I.

Women

Pardon my soap box,
But in my thirty years,
I've seen too many women falling.

Forsaking her own light
To conform to his world, so tight,
Taking on the kitchen's endless chores
To please his heart,
Wearing a mask of cheer
To offer him comfort, day or night,
Tiptoeing around his feelings
To attune to his mood,
Knowing when to speak, and when to be still,
To avoid unease,
Respecting all his boundaries set, in the name of
love,
To mold herself to his wishes, avoid fights,
Working on both fronts, carrying the burden
alone,
To fulfill society' script,
Reporting her pain,
To end up a victim, her voice unheard,
Cradling a newborn, in the quiet of the night,
To be a good mother while he's nowhere in
sight,

Bringing dedication and equal skills,
To suffer wage divide for all that she does.

Pardon my soapbox,
I'll carry on,
For I owe it to my daughter.
The world owes it too.

Through My Palestine Eyes

October 23, 2023

I've been witnessing our world crumble
For seventeen days in a row.
I look into my mother's tearful eyes
As she traces my name upon my skin.

All around us lies shattered,
It fell with a deafening roar.
Innocence vanished, to be no more.
Our homes reduced to rubble and dust -
With every tremor, we sit ready.
Once, the streets were full of children's laughter,
Now, only silent empty playgrounds around.

In my little brother's eyes,
I see the heaviness of a world unfair.

My mother softly sings "Lili Ou Noura,"
But the song, once soothing,
Now trembles with her vocal cords.
"Lili Ou Noura," once brought solace,
Now it stirs my soul.

Spiderweb

"Where's the spiderweb, Ms. Dalcheska?"
"Gone, I guess," I respond, and I don't look up.

My classroom is outside the building,
A trailer, one of the nine.
Right in front of it, on one of the columns,
A huge web and a spider hanging, we would see.

"It got killed, I think, or it went away," the
eight-year-old says,
"Maybe," looking at my schedule, I quickly add,
"The spider lived here for a while," another one
adds,
"Hey, like the geese!" they go on,
"Ms. Dalcheska, the geese think that the school
es su casa."
I agree, as I read the new email that was sent my
way,
I scribble down as we walk, another thing on my
list,
I forget they are eight-year-olds,
Innocent and playful,
And on my way back, I stop and see,
The spiderweb is not there.

To all the standards we adhere,
Chasing better scores,
BOGs, RtAs, Interims, ACCESS, EOGs to
administer.
In that bustle, little time do we have
To sit, talk, listen, love, and actually care.

The spider is gone, and if the eight-year-olds
Didn't show the web to me, I wouldn't have
known,
Of a life lived near my trailer.

Soul's Equinox

Born on summer's final day,
When summer's kiss meets autumn's gentle
morn,
In me, both summer's joy and autumn's yellow.

I am the evolving tides of the sea,
Unpredictable and fluid as a dream.

Emotions course through me like a river,
Their currents deep and wild,
From laughter's flow to depths of sorrow.

I am the whisper of summer's last breeze,
And the first leaf that flutters from the trees.

From sunrise's hope to midnight's embrace,
I am the bridge,
A tender touch before the abyss.

Two worlds in me collide,
Seeking a balance between day and night.

My Border Students

Guilford County Schools, 2023

As we dissect sentences into subject, verb,
object,
You teach me about life outside the border.
As we learn new vocabulary, 'ancestors' catches
your attention,
You tell me you long to see your grandparents
far away.

As we read about Pik's pok-a-tok challenge and
the quetzal's speed,
You compare it to a guardabarranco, and then I
learn.
As we tackle writing tasks, following all the
rules,
You say you find it hard to bridge the two
worlds in your head.

As 'heritage' rolls out our mouths, as if expelling
a breath of air,
You share memories of walking long and fraught
with uncertainty.
As we go through our lessons and all that they
entail,
I learn, and I am humbled by all that you carry.

The Art of Seduction in the City of Struga

The year 2013

Zero Celsius, each inhale feels like needles
piercing the lungs,
Yet, as always, a short figure-hugging dress,
Onyx high heels echoing on the cobbled streets,
Intense red lips, a statement of power,
You should've saved it for a better time.
This town bears the marks of entropy now.

The click-clacking in the icy 'charshija'
Takes me to a bar, one of the few left,
Dimly lit, more men than women there,
Men's inebriated attempts to follow turbo-folk
songs,
Grasping onto the lyrics as if they were a
lifeline,
A haze of cigarette smoke, spilled beer -
The air itself, a palpable presence.
"Hey, what're ya drinking?"

It's 2 a.m., and you should've been in bed by
now,
Is it his teetering walk?

Or the thud of his fist on the table?

On each visit, the regulars, and a few new,
younger faces,
Fresh entrants, brimming with energy and
enthusiasm.
I wouldn't trade places;
They've yet to clock in enough hours to spot all
the wear and tear.

I ditch the "Hey, what're ya drinking?" guy,
As usual, his demeanor changed -
"You're beautiful" turned into labeling,
I used to care when they resorted to offensive
vocabulary.

I settle into the backseat of a taxi,
The drivers always seek to break the silence,
Harmless, yet uninvited,
It feels like an intrusion into my tranquility.

I'm dropped off in front of my building,
Not paying attention to the passing car,
Its windows rolled down, a group of townsfolk
inside,
Towards me drift whistles and "Pretty", in
Albanian.

I lock my apartment door, disengaged.

Same old, yet ready to dive back into it,
Never thrilled.

Healing

Each moment, significant or mundane,
Seems to slip through my fingers,
Leaving a mark on my soul.

I cross the days on my calendar,
My time on Earth is marching,
I feel it most in the quiet of the night.

I think of what was waited for,
Experienced, lost, or missed,
All my relationships, from their inception to
their end.

I see a newborn, and a paradox emerges -
A bundle of life, full of promise,
Yet transient in the grand scope.

I diminish the weight of past triggers,
And I heal my soul by being true to myself,
No longer wounding, begging, pulling.

Because I, too,
Have suffered the atrocity of sunsets, Sylvia,
I, too, know the bottom.